Lost at home

BlueRose ONE
Stories Matter

First Published by

ISBN: 978-93-5704-876-7

Price: INR 180

BLUEROSE PUBLISHERS
www.bluerosepublishers.com
info@bluerosepublishers.com

+91 8882 898 89

This book is dedicated to my roots, to where and to whom I belong, to the hands that nurtured me , to the place that made me evolve and last but not the least to the genes that I inherited to be me!

11th October 2022

"Woke up upright...oops I need to feel if my back hurts. Ah not really. I put my right foot on the ground to stand up, and well, by now I know how to manage to do so even with the excruciating piercing pain in the right heel! Oh God it's almost six in the morning! My daughter is already on the cycle, happily tuned to the music with her ear phones on. The festivities being over, she is prepared to appear her weekly test at school today after mugging up the whole chapter on Renaissance, and must have repeatedly puked the entire whole thing about seven times by now!

I came back to her with a cup of warm milk which I do on regular basis, thinking it will give her all the vitamins and proteins and many more things which my Maa used to think it actually contained; so much so that she had taught us not to forget to rinse the cup with water once it is empty and gulp the same to ensure that no remnant of the milk is wasted. She still believes or rather is of the opinion that cow's milk was a super food and it superseded any other damn food on this universe!

Born in the family of the then rich Zamindars, my Maa is the youngest girl child of the eleven children of my grandparents (my Dadu and Dida as we call them). Honestly speaking, whatever I know of Dadu and Dida is entirely based on what was fed to our young inquisitive minds throughout the past decades by Maa. None of us, by which I mean the three of us, oh sorry, I always mean my two siblings and me when I say " the three of us"....none of us had the privilege to enjoy the affection, love and being of our maternal grandparents.

Late Advocate Manamohan DasGupta

Late Mrs. Chapala Dasgupta

Maa had lost her father when she was in the 2nd standard. One day while she was busy playing with her siblings and cousins in the courtyard the sound of women crying made her run inside the house in the direction of the sound, only to see that her father was lying still and listless. Her young innocent mind could not decipher the scene although... till she was told that her father was no more.

He had succumbed to some illness at a young age in the February of 1950. Till date I could not make out as to what he died of, but can only guess.

Maa shared memories of Dadu quite often to us while we sat chatting after meals at our large dining table in our open kitchen arrangement at home, whenever the strong punch of his being once ignited the urge in Maa to speak on the one and only Manomohan Dasgupta, an advocate by profession and a Zamindar by heredity. Maa remembers the purplish patch on one of his cheeks supposedly a haemangioma and would often say how clever and witty he was.

The stories of the famous Manu Das of Barisal, a province of the then undivided Bengal would make me feel proud of and in my imagination I had several pictures set which I visited and often revisited with so much warmth and happy-to-be-into-it feel; only to wake up the very next moment to feel the doom his demise had brought in. Dida was left all on her own with the big and unsurmountable responsibility of raising the kids, the youngest being just a toddler then!

The entire household seemed to crash. No doubt Dida was a strong and brave lady indeed hailing from a popular Zamindar family. Only the first few daughters of Dadu and Dida had been married off while Dadu was still alive, the eldest with aristrocratic beauty to a doctor who **in due course time** settled in Shillong, a hill station in Meghalaya in the north east of India; and the second, a dark and beautiful daughter to a school teacher in Kolkata. She herself was a teacher by profession and a tablist too. Just imagine a female tablist in those days !

The beautiful talented daughters had no difficulty in finding a perfect match for themselves. One settled in Ranchi, another got married in New Delhi and another in Dumdum in Kolkata. By the time the remaining five children grew into beautiful teens, Dida had fallen short of resources and was not able to keep up to the standards as before; but nothing could make her give up. I have often heard Maa say many a time as to how Dida handled the household, managed the Zamindari, maintained the social responsibilities and yet remained calm and composed and was duly loved and respected by the family, friends and society.

Chapala Dasgupta by marriage and emerging as Mejdi in the joint household of the Dasguptas, the daughter of Akshay Sen, who was a learned advocate of those times, had the tenacity to appear her unfinished school final along with my Maa, her tenth child. So many tales are haunting me now; now that my days are so full of leisure and the fact that I have opted for rest does not make me repent at all. I opted to come to a halt. Amidst so much of confusion, pain, panic and so on and so forth, I opted to come to a standstill in the truest sense of the term.

Being a doctor by profession life was never like this to me for the last few decades. Anybody can guess what the business is all about and the weight of the commitment. The length of hours spent in that, the tenacity it demands, not to mention the risks entangled in every bit of it. But the fact was that, I loved and welcomed each passing day with utter optimism and commitment, and as per my friends and colleagues say, I seemed to age gracefully in the profession until I chose to halt .

The Author

While still at school I believed or rather made to believe that I would make a good physician. The only reason was because once as a little child I showed the guts of nursing my grandmother's (Thakuma's) open wounds in the corner of one of her eyes (possibly the right), incurred from a fall, that too very intricately and bravely until she was fit. We all were Thakuma's pets, although I believed that she loved Piu, my younger sister, a little more than anybody else. Piu was almost 3 years younger to me. Born in 1ˢᵗ March 1975, she was sweet and sober and pretty faced with brownish black curls all over her shoulders, her angelic presence delighted any damn soul.

Baba, Maa and Thakuma

The Three Of Us

My little sister Piu on her toes in a birthday party in the neighborhood

Little me cuddled in Didi's lap who had just turned five!

After school I opted to do Medicine and securing a 19th rank in All Assam Entrance Test helped me to procure a seat in Guwahati Medical College and all I can say is, I basked in the grandeur of the Institute with every passing day. Honed by the experienced faculty who gave in their best to craft us to perfection, I feel lucky to be enabled for the function I had ethically sworn in! " Learn and deliver" had always been my passion; this mixed with a dash of honesty and empathy that I had genetically inherited from my parents helped me stay grounded and come out with flying colours in any service I got into. Working for the sake of name and fame, competing to show others low, had never been my cup of tea. Knowledge was always welcome but I never used it for self identity and never ever sought pleasure in self praise after each enlightenment. I like to live the present and learn from the past. I am not aware of what future has for me but definitely hope to dance to its tunes.

Today is Maa's birthday. She was born in Barisal now in Bangladesh during the festive season in 1942 in an affluent Zamindar family, no doubt with a silver spoon in her mouth. She was her mother's sixth girl child and very soon grew up to be her pet in no time. Her father was a reputed lawyer and took interest in playing footfall alongside managing their bulk of Zamindari. Theirs was a typical Bengali joint family and very well knit. Had it not been for the devastating communal riots years after Independence from British rule and 'Desh Bhaag' by the so-called scholars who happened to rule the then India, the entire family would not have been uprooted and instead peacefully flourished God knows to what extent in Barisal itself, retaining their identity at the place of origin.

At times I ponder as to what would have been the scenario had the case been so. whether or not would we exist is debatable, as things would have been totally different then. How I wish to go back to the astral world and get things corrected! But fortunately or unfortunately we are just puppets in the hands of destiny. I heard Maa say often how the town was ablaze during the riots. Humans turned into beasts their hearts and grey matter into the hands of the Dark Lords. It was a war won by the people hell bent to bring about whatever chaos they wanted, not at all considering the right and the wrong moves. How can the peace loving good souls survive a single second on such unpleasant circumstances? Fear, panic, anxiety for the impending doom clearly prevailed and made so many people from all spheres of life to decide on how to save their lives and come out safe from the manmade crisis.

Leaving behind her household intact, my Dida opted to shift in person(relocate) to India in the early 60s along with the young children she feared to lose at any moment, taking along some gold jewelleries hidden in a pot of "kheer", as Maa remembers, for she heard her Mom say so when asked by officials during routine checking on the way, to reach the City of Joy alive, unhurt and untouched, after being haunted day and night by the devastating situations that prevailed in Barisal.

Can anyone put his feet into her shoes and dare imagine the nerve anybody in a similar situation would need to have if encountered by the utter crisis people had been in then. Well, I just shiver and panic at the very thought of it and being witness to such a situation is beyond my imagination as I know my nerves pretty well.

Bravehearts were those who could come out of it and embrace whatever was in store for them in a different land. My salute to my Dida whom I have never seen, as I was born more than eight months after she died. The champion old lady my Dida. Thanks to her for successfully saving her life and those of her dear children without giving a second thought to doing something else.

The massive property and belongings and assests she left behind in the blink of an eye shows how unmaterialistic she was and all that mattered to her was her self respect and the safety and security of her beautiful children. I feel flattered and proud and honoured to claim and announce my bloodline, my lineage!

Now the question often peeks into my mind....had Dadu been alive then, would Dida make this move? Dadu would have been the decision maker then as to whether or not it was at all required to move out of the house leaving behind the generations old assests and he would have definitely weighed the risks and come to a conclusion with his alfa manlike instincts peppered with his experiences in the legal field. He would have cushioned the panic stricken household and protected and provided the lady of the house and the children the best way possible judiciously. But again destiny had something else in store- Dadu had been removed from the scene almost a decade ago, to leave the fate of his family in the clutches of destiny.

To my utter delight I thank Maa to have shared and relayed all her memories from the past every now and then when we chatted with her. Here I am, always very inquisitive and eager to learn about my roots, a the-then silent listener, now sharing with my readers the actual real story from the horse's mouth. When we feel connected to our past, we enjoy every moment talking about it again and again. Do you want to know who is the silent listener in my life now? It's my daughter I call her my one and only! The most precious thing that ever happened to me....

Now I often find myself talking to her in our leisure and I can see the curiosity and hunger in her to learn more of roots and I eagerly land up with my stories from the eventful past and she seems to absorb and imbibe all the matter and I enjoy the twinkle in her eyes as she listens. I enjoy the way she expresses her feeling of belonging and that too with extreme possessiveness. I can relate her feelings to mine, as to what I used to feel as a child when Maa kept on penning down her own childhood memories on our blank innocent faces as we sat making sighs and throwing comments geared up by innocent belongingness.

It gives me immense pleasure when I go back to munch my own days of past. We are three sisters as I said. My Didi, ie. my elder Sister who is almost 5 years elder to me, was my friend philosopher and guide all throughout my childhood days. My younger sister Piu was my all time cool buddy. Maa used to be more close to Didi and very friendly with her and both Piu and me used to be soul mates in that big house. Baba was a gem of a person and had it not been for his health issues he would have been the happiest person on earth with Maa by his side. He loved all and was loved by all. Plain and simple in his ways of thinking, with no manipulative cunningness, no hard feelings for a single human on earth, I think nobody equals him in my eyes till date. After his death I remember a very close family friend of ours saying, he was always dressed like a Sahib i.e. in proper formal wear throughout the day. It was then that it occurred to me that he actually used to be so.

My Baba was the gentlest man I have ever seen in my entire life. He was the only son to my Grandparents. He had an elder sister whom we called Pipi. My grandfather had been born and brought up in Dacca (Dhaka) in the then undivided Bengal, now in Bangladesh. He had been married to my Thakuma who was from Comilla district in Bangladesh. My Pipi and Baba were born in Dhaka. Grandpa and his younger brothers were real entrepreneurs. He along along with his brothers had established a number of Typewriting and Stenography institutes, the first one being in Dhaka itself, the second in Guwahati, Assam and another in Agarpara in West Bengal, the latter being looked after by two of his younger brothers.

When he decided to shift to Assam with his family, another brother of his used to run the Institute in Dhaka. He was Mr. W.C. Roy, who was so enterprising and talented that he is known to have begun the construction of shorthand in Assamese language but his work remained unfinished due to his untimely death. We still have the manuscripts in his own handwriting. My Didi has kept this legacy untold and is still taking care of it in the hope that it gets its due respect and recognition one day as she would always be mesmerised by this fact in her childhood as to what great initiative that person had taken. My grandpa Mr. K. P. Roy, along with his brother Mr. W. C. Roy had established the school in Guwahati in 1926. They were running the ones in Dacca and Assam with utmost care and passion.

When Grandpa relocated to Guwahati with Thakuma, Pipi and Baba in the early 50s with the surge of riots in Bangladesh, it was easier for him to run the school more efficiently as he did not have to travel anymore and the one in Dacca was well taken care of by his brother. But to their utter dismay things did not work the way they wanted. The great Partition ushered in the miseries along with it. Ill health followed by death of Mr. Woomesh Chandra Roy saw the end of the Institute in Dacca. My Grandpa was left alone in Assam as his other two brothers had opted to settle in Agarpara in West Bengal. None the less, there was no end to his optimism and passionate love for the profession and he happily ran the Institute named Commercial School (Estd.1926) the first of its kind in Assam and trained so many local youths and also his one and only son who had successfully mastered stenography as well as type writing in his teens.

My Dadu in the centre sitting with Thakuma in his left
and Baba still a bachelor then just behind him at his
Panbazar residence in Assam

Grandpa married his daughter to an engineer in Ranchi, my Pipa, Mr. D. K. Gupta. They had two children, a son and a daughter. Grandpa was loved and respected by all in Guwahati and he did not feel the need to recover whatever he had lost in Dacca; and the fact that his dear brother was no more, was enough to make him to choose to make himself at home in Assam only. Destiny was not kind to him either. He was diagnosed of Oesophageal Cancer in the mid fifties and succumbed to the disease leaving behind the entire family to mourn the massive loss. My father, although too young to take up the profession then, did his best to do so but he had to face the brunt of mental illness following the turn of events all of a sudden. He became the Principal of Commercial School and did his best to carry on the legacy.

He was married to Maa in 1965 on 31ˢᵗ July when he was almost 26 years old; arranged by a common family friend in New Alipore in West Bengal named Mr. Mohini Mukherjee, the wedding was held in Calcutta and Dida was happy to hand over her beautiful young daughter, named Madhuchhanda Dasgupta to the deserving groom. Maa had just graduated then from Basanti Devi College in Calcutta with History and had been selected for the higher studies in Presidency College but could not pursue the same as it was decided that she better get married for good. That ended her short stay of few years in Calcutta, to see a new beginning in the heart of Guwahati, Assam in the small cosy nuclear family headed by my Thakuma, who gladly welcomed her one and only daughter-in-law, whom she called Bouma, into the household handing her over the charge in no time. Maa won the hearts of all there and it did not take her much time to feel at home in the warm loving company of Baba and guardianship of Thakuma.

My paternal grandfather
Mr. K.P Roy

Little   Didi   in
Thakuma's lap

Didi's Rice ceremony

Little Didi in Dida's lap
during a visit to Kolkata
with beside them

Ma and Baba on a sunny day clicked on a cheerful mood

Baba and Didi during another visit to Kolkata.....

Myself as a toddler in Thakuma's lap....

Ma' Baba and Didi posing at a studio in Guwahati' Assam

Didi was born within a couple of years time and Thakuma was a proud grandma to the bubbly little girl. The family was again full of life and laughter and four years rolled by in no time. I was born in 1972 and grew up in utmost care of my loving parents, a possessive grandma, and a profoundly caring sister. But a brat I was as a toddler and the entire brunt was borne by the nanny and the full time helper and of course all present there had their own roles in my life as well. Very soon I was enrolled in an early morning school as the family was getting ready to welcome the third newcomer. An Aunt in the neighbourhood used to take me to the school in which she was a faculty, and I used to enjoy each and every day in the school to the fullest. My memories of The Bengali Girls' School are still fresh.

I remember when Maa had to be admitted to the hospital for a caesarean section for the third time, I was not yet three years old, Didi had opted to stay with Shundor Pishi, as Thakuma wouldn't be able to look after 2 kids and also she had Nitadi there to play with. Shundor Pishi was my Baba's maternal cousin and was the only close relative we had in Guwahati. We all enjoyed her love and affection towards us to the fullest. I was to stay with Thakuma and Baba at home. I can very well recollect the memories of that day when my Thakuma who was a widow and was not keen to touch or cook fish otherwise, following Grandpa's demise, was eagerly cooking some fish for Baba and me in Maa' absence, so that we are not deprived of the healthy protein even for a single day. What "milk" was to Maa, " fish" must have been to Thakuma.

She had compromised and chosen to come in terms with all her beliefs and traditions and resorted to doing what she felt was the need of the hour at that time.

She was one of the sweetest human beings I came across so far. She never ever complained of the tantrums we used to throw around her, often when she was in her room may be taking rest. Her vision was a bit compromised following a cataract surgery which was either not done properly or might have been a result of uncontrolled diabetes. She was our protector and shield and our only way out to escape from Maa and her strict rules, which got stricter with time.

Maa had no reach beyond the walls into Thakuma's room that's what I believed in childhood. I remember, Thakuma's four walled room used to be my shelter, which I often sought whenever I dared to break Maa's rules knowingly or unknowingly, and had the fear of getting scolded for the same. Whenever I returned home late after playing with friends in the evening, I would invariably choose to enter through Thakuma's room. ...pretending to have spent some quality time with her and then go to Maa; when asked the reason for being late (as we were to be back before dusk as per Maa's standing orders) I would resort to lying, saying that I had been back well ahead of time and was in Thakuma's room spending some quality time with her after that! I think Maa doesn't know about this mischief till date.

What all we did?! Whenever we annoyed Maa and she ran into fits of anger we would break into Thakuma's room to escape the brunt of the moment. The cushioning that awaited there had always been beyond imagination...those unforgettable moments of bliss !

And the games of Ludo with Thakuma, those were something I would long for. At times we used to get so much engrossed in playing that we had no idea what time it was until Maa called. Angels were we indeed, as no sooner she called than we jumped off saying goodbye to Thakuma. Interestingly, I think there were days when Thakuma did not feel like leaving a game half way; on one such occasion I remember her saying ".if you leave a game unfinished, you have chances of getting a headache". Thereafter I made it a point not to leave any game incomplete.

Whenever Piu and I preferred to play on our own, it would be in Thakuma's vicinity only. She would never get into our weird ways of playing ; be it her furnitures we aligned to play " train train" or be it one of her doors we chose to scribble on with chalks to play "teacher teacher" ! So much so, she used to make "luchi" and "begun bhajha" every time we conducted "putuler biye" with each other's dolls. This was our Thakuma and our childhood days ! Piu used to listen to whatever I said and whichever game plan I chalked out was not to be disobeyed nor asked for changes. Piu had never shown any traits of leadership ever.

She was very docile and submissive and never raised a voice of her own. At school, she grew up to be a chatter-box. All her primary report cards showed, "GOOD BUT VERY TALKITIVE " , which became a thing of concern for Maa. God knows what she blabbered about at school during classes that made the teachers complain. At times they would even call either of us i.e. Didi or me to complain in person. That same Piu is now just the opposite,- apparently a silent listener with a smile!!

If there were any uncalled visitor barging in at odd hours in our house we would prefer Piu to do the bit of talking. I would literally shun at the idea of doing this role and preferred to stay glued to books instead. Now it's just the other way round. It's me who does the talking and entertaining part in my household! Even if I don't want to do that badly, there is no way out

14th October 2022

Day before yesterday, it was Maa's 80th birthday. I always like celebrating birthdays, be it mine or any other person's. I feel happy to wish a person on his or her D'day. When asked by many, many a times , I couldn't say how and why I remember the birthdays. Rather so long I did not have time to ponder on the issue. Now when I have all the time in the world, I did some thinking on it, and feel that the reason behind must probably be that , I feel privileged to express my gratitude to the person concerned by wishing him or her on his or her birthday for the good role(if any or may be many) he or she is playing by virtue of his or her life on earth. I take my turn to wish a safe and blissful year ahead. Wishing on birthdays has nothing to do with hard feelings if any, nothing to do with people whom I like or dislike, nothing related to any selfish motive, nothing that I can think of .

Maa opted to stay all alone in Guwahati, Assam at our Panbazar residence after Baba's demise. Although with age she has acquired few age related problems like senile dementia, hearing issues, decreasing strength etc., she retains the intelligence and independent nature and optimism. She hates to get displaced from her home anymore and insists on staying on her own so what all on herself. Till date she manages the daily chores without anybody's help and infact opts to do so to keep herself engaged and happy.

 The first bout of Covid she had, literally went unnoticed by her but the post Covid consequences had taken a toll on her. By God's grace we three sisters managed to save her from the clutches of Corona.

Today I started packing for a small trip we had been planning so long. We had paid an advance for this trip two and a half years ago in February 2020. With the onset of Covid Pandemic in March 2020 when things went haywire, we could not even think of going anywhere. Now, after the two long years of absolute surrender to the virus, that we have managed to get shielded to its weird unpredictable attacks, we thought it wise to reschedule the trip at our convenience.

Packing for holidays has always been my passion. Now it has turned into the best pastime. It acts as a mood elevator for me. So much so that I often resort to packing and seek the pleasure out of it! Oh the very thought of travelling and moving to a different place gives me a kick... I think many people are aware of it by now.

Recently I had to rush to my Uncle-in-law's place on hearing about his ill health that required immediate hospital admission. Being a doctor and the only nearest relative available, I was to go and stay with my Aunt-in-law who happens to be terminally ill, bravely fighting Parkinson's. I just picked the suitcase I had packed once for a stay during the summer for 3 to 4 days that got cancelled due to some reason and reached Highland Park in no time. How glad I was that I wasted no time in packing at all and could be of help at the same time... that was a day when people around me were in praises for the passion I harboured! Eager to pack any time!

It's 18th of October 2022. Woke up to the alarm which my daughter usually sets up if she has school. I like that song and intended to keep on listening to it but my daughter wanted me to snooze it off as she hated to get reminded of the fact that she had to spring out of her cosy couch and be ready for the routine pick-up from the neighbourhood in an hour or so. Probably the very thought of leaving the sleep unfinished and literally gearing up to make up her mind for the morning chores which included brushing, having a glass of water, warming up, having a glass of milk before taking a good bath and then dressing up for school after a healthy sumptuous breakfast, was what gave rise to the intense need of having the alarm switched off immediately.

What "milk" is to Maa and " fish" was to Thakuma, I guess " eggs and bananas" are to me. Oh my God! You can't imagine how I visualize the proteins and vitamins being delivered into whoever takes those without any resistance. God forbid, if by chance anybody expresses his or her displeasure and reluctance in having those at breakfast to my surprise, I feel I have failed to arm them with the required proteins and vitamins for the day! The feel-good and assurance of good health those gave, matter the most to me and looking out for any alternative seems to be a hard and time wasting task. You should see the disappointment I go through upon being shown a 'NO' placard on serving a plate of toast with sunny side ups and a big banana at breakfast by whosoever it is! I blame this on the acquired trait of a unique perception which manifests by default! Even my household helper is aware of this fact and cleverly tries to deal with me to escape the brunt.

20th October 2022

Come Thursday and see what plans are there in my 'Things to do ' list.

The A.C. guy had complained of an 'earthing' problem while attending to the air conditioners with perennial issues the other day and had asked me to get a thorough check up done by the electrician. Our most trustworthy electrician had given us an appointment in the evening and it took him three long hours combing the issues and since then my house seems to be in a total mess. Had it been my usual working days like I used to have before, I would have shunned at the emergence of such unwelcome troubles. But chill.... I have completed almost more than three months of full rest and isolation from things that get on to my nerves and am now no more vulnerable to the painstaking trouble-shoots that would otherwise mess up a busy routined schedule. Oh yes.... What if the dressing table has been pulled forwards from its usual location in an attempt to expose the A.C. main switch, only to show up the months old layers of dust and cobwebs behind it What if the huge refrigerator has been pushed to the other side to bring to light the dusty back and the nasty floor beneath, which needs to be attended to by the maid when she comes next day.

Now that I am home , things are different. Had it been on my usual working days, I would receive a call from Rina, my most trustworthy helper, in the midst of examining a prospective blood donor, delivering her concern over the top of her voice as to what has led to the state of affairs at home. Would have to calm her down while the donor remains seated in front of me. No such thing is going to happen today, now that I am there in person to explain her the entire matter.

After an elaborate cleaning conducted by Rina today, I could take a sigh of relief.

In the evening I need to show our duplex for sale to Mr. Tiwari who had called up yesterday for fixing a time. His lawyer son would be visiting the site on his behalf to make summations on the state of the property and convey the same to his father. Now that I am able to sit without pain even on low lying car seats, it is no longer a botheration to run on such errands once in a while. All I need to do is hire an OLA or Uber and take Khokan our gardener along to finish off the work in an hour's time.

Come what may, after judging the authenticity of the buyers we are left with no choice but to be present during each and every visit; who knows who might actually fall for Adelina and we just need to give in, handing her over to them like giving away an asset, which costs something more than your two decades of hard - earned money, hard passionate work, emotions attached there in, born out of the dreams within.

Back home there will be some guests to entertain and have dinner with. A busy day ahead indeed … I am thankful to my physician to have made me able to bring me back to my otherwise active form. But I am still not sure whether it will be wise to catch up with my original gear and back in my mind still opt to stay home away from the hustle and bustle of life…. the must-be s, the do s and don't s and all those stuff that get on your nerves in everyday life. Because I know pretty well the tuning one needs to deal with such chores.

It is nice to think and cherish that the holidays that had been postponed for more than two long years due to Covid virus at our doorstep, have actually neared , and all of us who are going there seem to be more than excited . The holiday momentum has picked up at each and everyone's house. My cousin and his wife has not yet packed though, but Dada seemed hyperexcited with all his what's app 'good mornings' which proves that his mind is already flying away from its usual abode. My daughter's friend and her parents are equally elated in between their busy schedule as the day comes closer. HOLIDAYS.... The passion of our lives, the irreplaceable food for the body and mind, the one and only way to bring about an end to the little miseries of everyday life. It cures and uplifts us from within.

The memories we carry back knows no bounds. Each and every second captured and consumed, ready to be replayed in our thoughts whenever the mind fleets to those far off lands...lands that exist in real and where we had set our foot on! That's where lies the charm and adventure...not to mention the warmth of the company we are in...people known or unknown to you, becomes a part of the days spent!

For my readers, who must be curious by now, our destination this time will be the fascinating Andamans day after tomorrow onwards. We are already in a get-set-go mode and had it not been for my daughter's weekly test today, she would have bunked school on some very silly ground just to enjoy the present momentum in the air and I would be left with no other choice than to give in to her childish pranks and tantrums rather than be able to jot down my excitement and feel good to you.

My husband who is a devoted surgeon and a total workaholic has also picked up the magical compulsiveness of getting into the mood of packing and seems to be infused with the extra bout of energy with the holiday spirit in the air! He in fact sounded overwhelmed from yesterday itself and has already finished winding up at the work front making himself fully available without any impending commitments, well ahead of the upcoming trip. The workaholic has geared up to go off- work...gosh!

www.ingramcontent.com/pod-product-compliance
Lightning Source LLC
LaVergne TN
LVHW091133180726
843490LV00008B/2946